SIMPLE MACHINES

RAMPS

Nancy Dickmann

BROWN BEAR BOOKS

Published by Brown Bear Books Ltd
4877 N. Circulo Bujia
Tucson, AZ 85718
USA

and

Leroy House
436 Essex Rd
London N1 3QP
UK

ISBN 978-1-78121-400-8 (library bound)
ISBN 978-1-78121-430-5 (paperback)

Library of Congress Cataloging-in-Publication Data available on request

Text: Nancy Dickmann
Design Manager: Keith Davis
Picture Manger: Sophie Mortimer
Editorial Director: Lindsey Lowe
Children's Publisher: Anne O'Daly

Manufactured in the United States of America
CPSIA compliance information: Batch#AG/5608

Picture Credits
The photographs in this book are used by permission and through the courtesy of:

Front Cover: Alamy: Susan Norwood bl; Shutterstock: main.
Interior: Alamy: Hero Images Inc 21b. Susan Norwod 16; Dreamstime: Duccio 4, Juriah Mosin 20-21, Michael Pelin 21t; Getty Images: Brian Mitchell 16–17; istockphoto: 1, 20b, Steven Allen 12, Kall9 10–11, Willowpix 8–9; Shutterstock: 4–5, 10, 14–15, Mario hagen 14; Thinkstock: istockphoto 6, 6–7, 12–13, 18, 18–19, 20l.

All other artwork and photography © Brown Bear Books.

t-top, r-right, l-left, c-center, b-bottom

Brown Bear Books has made every attempt to contact the copyright holder. If you have any information please contact: licensing@brownbearbooks.co.uk

Websites
The website addresses in this book were valid at the time of going to press. However, it is possible that contents or addresses may change following publication of this book. No responsibility for any such changes can be accepted by the author or the publisher. Readers should be supervised when they access the Internet.

Words in **bold** appear in the Useful Words on page 23.

Contents

What Is a Ramp?

A ramp is a flat surface that is raised at one end. Ramps are sometimes called inclined planes. Ramps are simple **machines**. They make it easier to raise things.

WOW!

A path can be a ramp. It makes it easier to climb up a steep hill.

Objects move up a ramp. They also move down a ramp. Ramps can be fun! A slide is a ramp. It lets you slide to the ground.

What Are Machines?

A **machine** helps us do work. Using a machine can make it easier to lift heavy objects. Machines let us spread a **force** over a longer distance.

This is a parking garage. It has a long ramp. The ramp helps cars drive to the top.

Some machines are complicated. They have lots of parts. Some of the parts are simple machines. They work together.

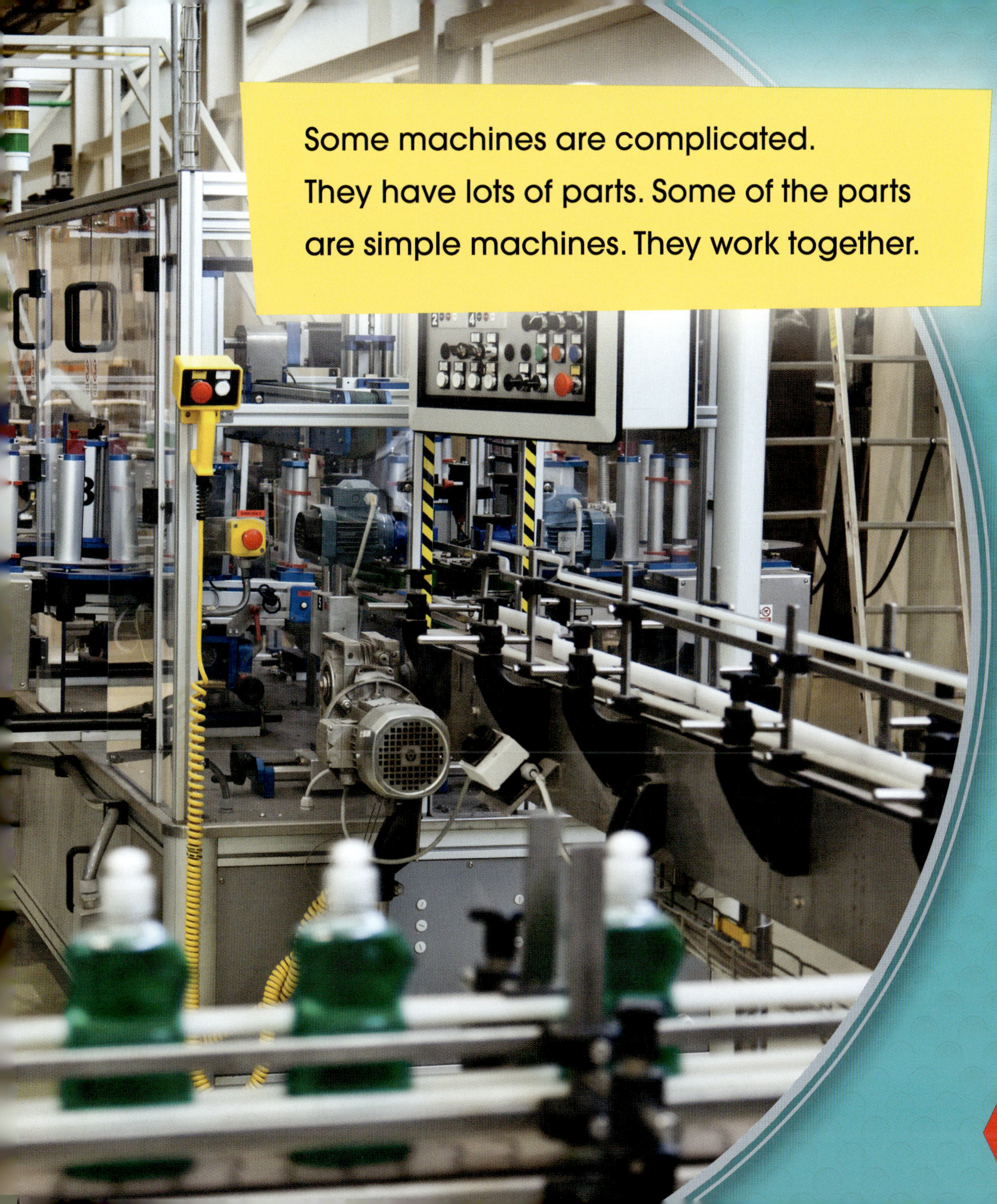

Ramps and Forces

A **force** is a push or a pull. We use force to lift something. A ramp spreads the force over a longer distance. It makes it easier to lift an object.

Forces

A ramp can help raise a heavy **load**.

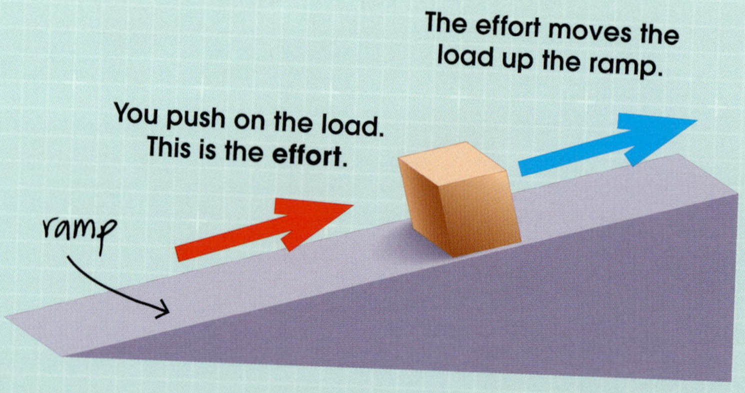

Lifting an object straight up is hard.
A ramp makes it easier to lift heavy things.
You can pull or push them up the ramp.

How Steep?

Some ramps are steep.
You need more **force** to push something up a steep ramp.
But you do not have to push it very far.

WOW!

A staircase is a ramp.
It is easier to climb from one floor to the next than to jump!

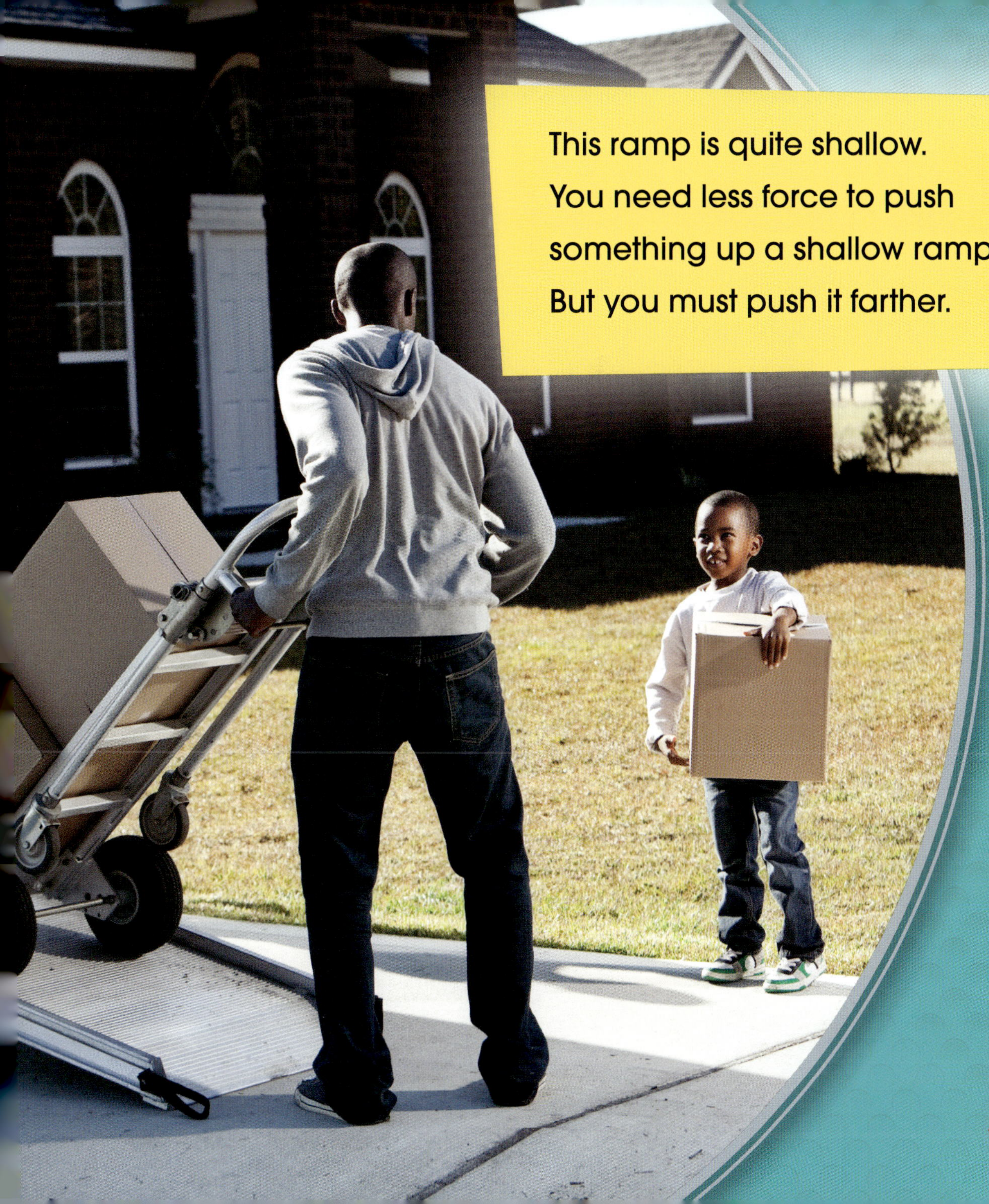

This ramp is quite shallow.
You need less force to push
something up a shallow ramp.
But you must push it farther.

Ramps in the Past

No one knows who invented ramps. Ancient people used them. Ramps helped them move heavy objects. Natural ramps helped them climb hills.

WOW!

The Romans made this ramp. They built it almost 2,000 years ago. It helped their army march to the top.

People in ancient Egypt used ramps. The pyramids are made of huge stone blocks. Workers pulled the blocks up ramps. When they were finished, they took the ramps down.

Ramps Today

Ramps have different jobs. A roof can be a ramp. Heavy snow slides off it. A dump truck can be a ramp. The bed lifts up and makes a ramp. The **load** slides down safely.

WOW!

Airplanes have slides. The slides are for an **emergency**. Passengers escape down the slide.

This road is a long ramp. It zigzags up the steep hill. A car drives farther on the road. But it is easier than driving straight up the hill.

Everyday Ramps

We use ramps at home and at play. Skate parks have ramps. It is fun to ride up and down on them. A ladder is a kind of ramp. It helps us climb higher with less effort.

Ramps can help pets. They make it easier to climb into a car.

Wheelchairs cannot go up or down stairs. They use ramps instead. They can roll easily up or down a ramp.

Compound Machines

Ramps are simple machines. **Compound machines** are more complicated. They are made of different machines. The parts work together.

An escalator is a moving staircase. It is a kind of ramp. Machines inside help it move.

A conveyor belt is a compound machine. It moves materials from one place to another. Its slope is a ramp. Inside are wheels and **pulleys**. Together they make the ramp move.

Spot the Ramp!

Can you find the ramps in these pictures?

1

3

2

4

5

Try It!

Make your own ramp. Can you find the angle that works best?

You will need:

- **large hardback book**
- **about a dozen more books**
- **jar of marbles (or other heavy weight)**
- **piece of string**

1. Make a short stack of books.

2. Lay the large book so that one end is on the floor and the other rests on top of the stack. This is your ramp.

3. Tie the string around the jar of marbles. This is your load.

4. Place the jar at the bottom of the ramp and use the string to pull it to the top.

5. Add more books to make the ramp steeper. Try pulling the load again.

Is it easier to pull the load up a steep ramp or a shallow one?

Useful Words

compound machine A machine that is made up of smaller machines.

effort The force required to move an object.

emergency Something that happens suddenly. It is often dangerous.

force A push or a pull.

load An object that you use force to move.

machine Something that helps us do work. Machines use energy to do a job.

pulleys Simple machines. They have a wheel with a rope running over it. Pulleys help lift heavy objects.

Answers to page 20–21: Did you spot the ramps?
1. The conveyor belt; **2.** the wheelchair ramp;
3. the waterslide; **4.** the road; **5.** the truck's ramp.

Find out More

Websites

www.idahoptv.org/sciencetrek/topics/simple_machines/facts.cfm

www.livescience.com/49106-simple-machines.html

www.msichicago.org/play/simplemachines/

Books

Ramps Kay Manolis, Bellwether Media 2016

Ramps and Wedges Sian Smith, Heinemann-Raintree 2012

Making Machines with Ramps and Wedges Chris Oxlade, Raintree 2015

Index